How to be a WWE Superstar

Written by
Steve Pantaleo

Penguin Random House

Editor Pamela Afram
Designer Sunita Gahir
Cover designed by James McKeag
Senior Editor Tori Kosara
Senior Designer Nathan Martin
Pre-production Producer Siu Yin Chan
Senior Producer Lloyd Robertson
Managing Editor Paula Regan
Managing Art Editor Jo Connor
Publisher Julie Ferris
Art Director Lisa Lanzarini
Publishing Director Simon Beecroft

Reading Consultant Linda B. Gambrell, Ph.D

First American Edition, 2017
Published in the United States by DK Publishing
1450 Broadway, Suite 801, New York, New York 10018

Page design copyright © 2020 Dorling Kindersley Limited
DK, a Division of Penguin Random House LLC
21 10 9 8 7
007–299074–Aug/2017

A catalog record for this book is available from the Library of Congress.

ISBN 978-1-4654-6288-6 (Hardcover)
ISBN 978-1-4654-6287-9 (Paperback)

DK books are available at special discounts when purchased in bulk for sales promotions,
premiums, fund-raising, or educational use. For details, contact: DK Publishing SpecialMarkets,
1450 Broadway, Suite 801, New York, New York 10018
SpecialSales@dk.com

Printed and bound in China

For the curious

www.dk.com
www.wwe.com

2

Contents

Welcome to WWE!

WWE Superstars are some of the toughest athletes on the planet.

Finn Bálor

Roman Reigns

More than 100 Superstars compete each week on *RAW* and *SmackDown Live*. Only the best competitors win big prizes called championships.

What makes a WWE Superstar?

No two WWE Superstars are alike. Some rely on strength to win a match. Others use moves that surprise their foes. Look at Seth Rollins fly!

A big personality is also important.
Sasha Banks likes to make the
crowd cheer. Her nickname is
The Boss.

Getting ready

Superstars are always preparing for the next match. They aim to work harder than their rivals. Dolph Ziggler trains every day. He lifts weights and does box jumps to stay strong.

WWE Performance Center

New competitors train at WWE's Performance Center. They learn the skills they need to become WWE Superstars.

There are seven practice rings inside the Performance Center. WWE athletes exercise and practice their moves here.

Match ready

Superstars battle in several types of matches. In a Ladder Match, Superstars must reach the top and be the first to grab a hanging object. At 20 feet high, WWE's ladders are taller than a giraffe!

In a Steel Cage Match, competitors battle inside a giant cage. The tall sides of the cage make it difficult for Superstars to get in or out.

Making an entrance

Superstars arrive for matches in style. The Rock excited the crowd at *WrestleMania* 32 with a fiery entrance.

Cheering crowds

Superstars love to get the crowd roaring. They come up with fun ways to get cheers, or even boos!

The New Day are always popular with the crowd. They wear bright outfits. Xavier Woods plays a trombone to excite the audience.

Signature moves

Some Superstars use special
moves to help them win a match.
These are called signature moves.

Becky Lynch tugs on her
opponent's arm to make her give
up. Neville performs his Red
Arrow move. He twists in midair
and crashes down on a fallen foe.

Finishing moves

Many Superstars use special moves to help them end a match and win it.

F-5

Brock Lesnar twists like a powerful tornado to throw opponents off his shoulders.

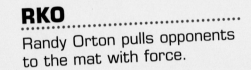

RKO
Randy Orton pulls opponents to the mat with force.

SHARPSHOOTER
Natalya uses this move to make opponents give up. Her uncle, Bret "Hit Man" Hart, made this move famous.

Role of a manager

Managers give Superstars advice before and during a match. They tell Superstars what to do in the ring to win.

Darren Young with his manager, Bob Backlund.

Manager Maryse does not agree
with the referee's decision. She
wants him to change his mind
so that The Miz can win.

Rules of the ring

WWE referees make sure Superstars follow the rules. A competitor can be disqualified if they try to cheat.

There are a lot of rules to follow. For example, Superstars cannot touch a referee. They are also not allowed to leave the ring for more than 10 seconds.

The referee reminds Jack Swagger to obey the rules or he will be disqualified!

Bending the rules

Some WWE Superstars do not follow any of the rules. Here are some sneaky moves to watch out for!

SNEAK ATTACK

Superstars sometimes surprise their opponent with a sneak attack as they enter the ring.

HIDDEN OBJECT

Some competitors try to hide an object in their outfit to use in the match.

PULLING TIGHTS

A Superstar might try to pin an opponent by pulling on their tights. This is not allowed!

Alexa Bliss surprises her rival, Becky Lynch, from behind.

Facing rivals

Many Superstars have a rival.
A rival is someone they are always
trying to beat. John Cena and
Randy Orton both became
Superstars in 2002. They have
been rivals ever since.

John Cena tries his best to win in every match. He knows Randy will try his hardest, too.

Know your rivals

A WWE Superstar must know who their enemies are. Then they will know how to beat them.

NAME:
Dean Ambrose

LIKES:
Danger

DISLIKES:
Wearing tights

WATCH OUT FOR:
Unexpected moves

NAME:
John Cena

LIKES:
Hard work

DISLIKES:
Taking shortcuts

WATCH OUT FOR:
Determination. John Cena never gives up.

NAME:
Charlotte Flair

LIKES:
Her WWE family history

DISLIKES:
Not getting what she wants

WATCH OUT FOR:
Sneak attacks from her friends

NAME:
Roman Reigns

LIKES:
People who say he can't do something. He will prove them wrong!

DISLIKES:
Big mouths

WATCH OUT FO
His powerful Superma Punch

Tag team power

Two or more Superstars can join
forces and become a tag team.
The Usos are twin brothers.
They have always been a team.

Sheamus and Cesaro did not like each other when they teamed up. The two Superstars soon learned to work together.

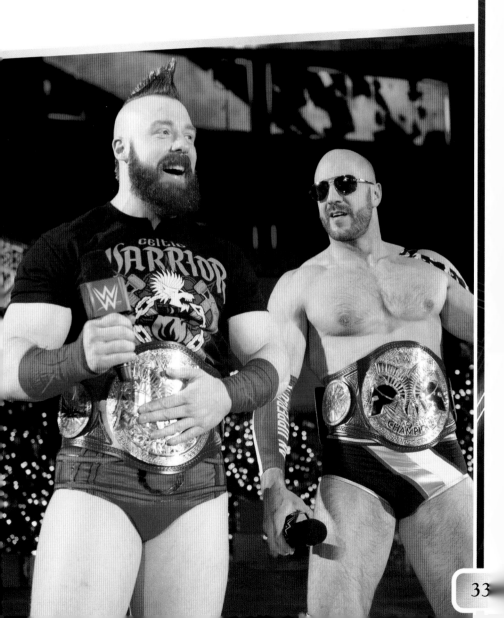

Terrific tournaments

A tournament is made up of many matches. To win the tournament, Superstars must win every match.

The Authors of Pain beat the Bollywood Boyz.

Next, The Authors of Pain win against No Way Jose and Rich Swann.

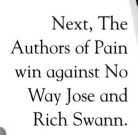

The Authors of Pain win the tournament.

Superstars must be ready for any opponent. It is hard to stay strong during so many matches. Finally, the winners get a shiny trophy!

Championships

Every Superstar wants to win a championship. They are the biggest prizes in WWE. Superstars work very hard to win them.

Dolph Ziggler wins the Intercontinental Championship.

Winning a championship makes a Superstar's hard work worth it. The champions love to cheer and celebrate!

Rhyno and Heath Slater win the *SmackDown* Tag Team Championship.

Becky Lynch wins the *SmackDown* Women's Championship.

Legendary champions

Some Superstars have won a championship more than once.

NAME:

Shawn Michaels

TITLE:

WWE Championship

NUMBER OF TIMES WON:

Three

NAME:

Sting

TITLE:

World Heavyweight
Championship

**NUMBER OF
TIMES WON:**

Six

NAME:

Trish Stratus

TITLE:

Women's Championship

**NUMBER OF
TIMES WON:**

Seven

Getting to *WrestleMania*

Every Superstar wants to compete at *WrestleMania*. It is WWE's biggest and most popular event.

Millions of people watch every *WrestleMania* match. It is a chance to see the best Superstars perform.

Seth Rollins at *WrestleMania 31*

Becoming a champion

It is exciting to be a champion. The crowd always cheers for the winner. However, a champion must work hard to keep a championship.

Rivals will want to take the title for themselves. Just like John Cena, true champions never give up!

Quiz

1. What is Sasha Banks's nickname?

2. Who plays a trombone?

3. What is Neville's signature move?

4. How many practice rings are there in the WWE Performance Center?

5. Who makes sure Superstars follow the rules during a match?

6. Which Superstar has a powerful Superman Punch move?

7. How high are the ladders in a Ladder Match?

8. How many times has Trish Stratus won the Women's Championship?

Answers on page 48

Glossary

athlete
A person who is skilled at a sport.

audience
The people watching an event.

competitor
Someone who takes part in a contest.

disqualified
When someone loses a match because they have broken a rule.

opponent
Someone who competes against someone else in a contest.

personality
The qualities that make each person who they are.

signature move
A Superstar's best move in the ring.

tournament
A series of contests for a prize.

A LEVEL FOR EVERY READER

This book is a part of an exciting four-level reading series to support children in developing the habit of reading widely for both pleasure and information. Each book is designed to develop a child's reading skills, fluency, grammar awareness, and comprehension in order to build confidence and enjoyment when reading.

Ready for a Level 2 (Beginning to Read) book

A child should:

- be able to recognize a bank of common words quickly and be able to blend sounds together to make some words.
- be familiar with using beginner letter sounds and context clues to figure out unfamiliar words.
- sometimes correct his/her reading if it doesn't look right or make sense.
- be aware of the need for a slight pause at commas and a longer one at periods.

A valuable and shared reading experience

For many children, reading requires much effort, but adult participation can make reading both fun and easier. Here are a few tips on how to use this book with a young reader:

Check out the contents together:

- read about the book on the back cover and talk about the contents page to help heighten interest and expectation.
- discuss new or difficult words.
- chat about labels, annotations, and pictures.

Support the reader:

- give the book to the young reader to turn the pages.
- where necessary, encourage longer words to be broken into syllables, sound out each one, and then flow the syllables together; ask him/her to reread the sentence to check the meaning.
- encourage the reader to vary her/his voice as she/he reads; demonstrate how to do this if helpful.

Talk at the end of each book, or after every few pages:

- ask questions about the text and the meaning of the words used—this helps develop comprehension skills.
- read the quiz at the end of the book and encourage the reader to answer the questions, if necessary, by turning back to the relevant pages to find the answers.

Series consultant, Dr. Linda Gambrell, Distinguished Professor of Education at Clemson University, has served as President of the National Reading Conference, the College Reading Association, and the International Reading Association.

Index

Answers to the quiz on page 44:
1. The Boss 2. Xavier Woods 3. Red Arrow 4. Seven 5. The referee
6. Roman Reigns 7. 20 feet 8. Seven